JUST

CW00375395

Other titles in this series

Just Enough German

Just Enough French

Just Enough Spanish

Just Enough Hindi

Just Enough Italian

Francesca Logi

Hugo's Language Books Limited

'Just Enough Italian' is also available in a pack with two cassettes:
ISBN 0 85285 227 4

Written by
Francesca Logi

Edited by
Jenny Yoboué

Illustrations by Sonia Robinson

Set in Palatino and Optima by
Andrew Burrell

Printed and bound in Great Britain by
Scotprint

Contents

1	Getting Started	9
2	Ordering Drinks	17
3	Finding Accommodation	27
4	Meeting People	41
5	Around Town	49
6	Travelling Around	57
7	Out and About	71
8	Out for a Meal	81
9	Shopping	89
10	Emergency!	97

Key to Exercises — 105

Mini–Dictionary — 111

    Italian–English — 111

    English–Italian — 117

Index — 123

Preface

If you are planning a trip to Italy, whether on business or on holiday, **Just Enough Italian** is the ideal quick and easy course to work through before you go. The course offers much more than a phrase book or travel pack, giving you the confidence to have a go at speaking some Italian yourself, as well as understanding what's being said to YOU. Your trip will be so much more enjoyable if you can communicate with the Italians, and they will appreciate the effort you make to speak their language.

To get you started, the first chapter introduces you to the alphabet and the essentials of Italian pronunciation. The remaining chapters contain lively, realistic dialogues, practice sections for you to try out what you have learned, 'Streetwise' sections with information and tips on different aspects of Italian life, Language Notes and exercises – with answers in the key at the back of the book! There is also a two-way Mini-Dictionary at the back of the book – handy for quick reference.

If you have the cassettes, you will find that these greatly enhance the learning process, bringing to life the dialogues and making exercises more fun.

We hope you enjoy **Just Enough Italian** and have a pleasant trip!

1 Getting Started

THE ALPHABET

The Italian alphabet is composed as follows, the names of the letters being given in an imitative form of pronunciation explained below. You'll need to know how to say these letters if you ever have to spell out your name – it's no good saying J–O–N–E–S because Italians won't understand J, which they call "ee loong-ah".

A	*ah*	**J**	*ee loong-ah*	**S**	*ehs-say*
B	*bee*	**K**	*kahp-pah*	**T**	*tee*
C	*chee*	**L**	*ehl-lay*	**U**	*oo*
D	*dee*	**M**	*ehm-may*	**V**	*voo*
E	*eh*	**N**	*ehn-nay*	**W**	*dop-pe-ah voo*
F	*ehf-fay*	**O**	*o*	**X**	*eeks*
G	*jee*	**P**	*pee*	**Y**	*eep-se-lon*
H	*ahk-kah*	**Q**	*koo*	**Z**	*zayt-tah*
I	*ee*	**R**	*ehr-ray*		

Note that the letters J, K, W, X and Y are quite rare in Italian.

PRACTISE PRONOUNCING!

If you can, use the tapes which go with this book – they will be very useful in learning the correct pronunciation.

In Italian all letters are sounded, therefore you will have to say them all. Read the notes below, and practise your pronunciation as often as possible. Practise it aloud, not muttering to yourself; in your mind's ear you may think you've got it right, but mind and vocal chords sometimes don't link up too well! If you cannot use the tapes, our system of imitated pronunciation (where the Italian is transcribed into English sound syllables should help you.

IMITATED PRONUNCIATION

The system should be self-evident, but bear in mind:

ah   sounds like "a" in "fast" but is shorter than in English.

o   sounds like "o" in "order" or "au" in "caught".

eh   sounds like "e" in "pen", shorter than "ay" in "say".

n'y   sounds like "ni" in "onion".

l'y   sounds like "lli" in "million".

rr   (sometimes r-r) should be rrolled like a Scottish "r".

Italian words all end in a vowel and are generally stressed on the last-but-one syllable. Those which are stressed on the last vowel (hence the last syllable) are marked with a grave (`) accent on that vowel. The vowel combinations –ia, –io and –ie at the end of a word are normally considered as a single syllable, so the stress falls on the preceding syllable (**Venezia** [veh-_neh_-tsiah], **doppio** [_dop_-peeo]). Some words are stressed earlier than the last-but-one syllable (**bellissimo** [behl-_lees_-see-mo). Abnormal stresses such as these will not be shown in the book; listen carefully to the tape if you have it.

VOWEL SOUNDS

The pronunciation of vowels (A, E, I, O, U) is different from the English. Generally, Italian vowels are not slurred or drawled, but are sounded in a distinctive way. Practise pronouncing these words:

a   like "a" in "ask" –

    pasta [pahs-tah]
    pizza [peets-sah]
    mamma [mahm-mah]

e   like "e" in "pen" –

    bene [beh-neh]
    ecco [ehk-ko]

i   like "ea" in "tea" or "ee" in "see" –

    si [see]
    vino [vee-no]

o   like "o" in "not" –

    no [no]
    sole [so-leh]
    ecco [ehk-ko]

u   like "oo" in "cool" –

    uno [oo-no]
    una [oo-nah]

CONSONANTS

The following Italian consonants are pronounced approximately as in English:

b   d   f   l   m   n   p   t   v

The letters j, k, w, x and y aren't found in Italian, except when they occur in foreign words such as the ubiquitous **jeans**, **jogging**, **weekend** and **whisky**. See also **h** below.

Some letters and some combinations of letters need special attention:

ca, **co**, **cu** and **c** followed by a consonant:
    pronounced like the "c" in "cat" –
    carota [kah-rrot-ah]
    cocco [kock-o]
    cubo [koo-bo]
    crostino [kross-tee-no]

Remember especially that **ch** comes into this same category:
    chilo [kee-lo]
    perché [pairr-kay]

ce, **ci**:
    pronounced like the "ch" in "chat" –
    celeste [chay-less-tay]
    cintura [chin-toor-rah]

ga, go, gu, and **g** followed by a consonant:
   pronounced like the "g" in "get" –
   gatto [gaht-to]
   golfo [gol-fo]
   guasto [gwass-to]

Remember also that **gh** is in this group:
   alberghi [ahl-bairr-ghe]
   traghetto [trah-get-to]

ge, gi:
   pronounced like the "j" in "jeep" –
   gelato [jay-lah-to]
   giro [jeer-ro]

gl:
   pronounced like "ll" in "million" –
   biglietto [bee-l'yet-o]
   luglio [loo-l'yo]

gn:
   pronounced like "ni" in "onion" –
   bagno [bah-n'yo]
   signora [see-n'yor-rah]
   cognome [ko-n'yo-may]

h:
   is never pronounced. It occurs in only a few Italian words as an initial letter to differentiate between **ho** ("I have") and **o** ("or"), **hanno** ("they have") and **anno** ("year"). Inside a word it may alter the pronunciation of the preceding letter (**alberghi** would sound as [ahl-bairr-jee] if the **h** was absent), so be careful.

qu:
   is like "qu" in "quick" –
   qui [kwee]
   quale [kwah-lay]
   quadro [kwah-dro]

r:

is rolled, rrr –
rosso [rross-so]
sera [say-rrah]
albergo [ahl-bairr-go]

s before consonants or when double, and at the beginnings of words:
pronounced sharp, as in "see" –
misto [miss-to]
posso [pos-soh]
strada [strah-dah]

s when between two vowels:
pronounced like the"z" in "lazy' –
casa [kah-zah]
Pisa [pee-zah]

sc when followed by **e** or **i**:
pronounced like "s" in "sure"
scena [shay-nah]
pesce [pay-shay]
sciare [she'ah-ray]

sc when followed by **a, o, u** or **h**:
is like "sk" in "skin" –
scarpa [skarr-pah]
sconto [skon-to]
scultura [skool-toor-rah]
scheggia [sked-jah]

z:

pronounced like "ts" in "gutsy", but can sometimes be softer (more like "dz"). There aren't any precise 'rules' so the best advice is aim for a middle way –
grazie [grah-tse'ay]
pranzo [prahn-dzo]
mezzo [med-dzo]
terrazza [tair-rats-sah]

Remember that double consonants are emphasised and pronounced as if there were a short pause between them. If you have the tapes, listen to the difference: **ditta, dita; sonno,**

sono. In words like **gnocchi**, **scheggia**, **maggiore**, the first letter of a double consonant gives way to the second.

BASIC EXPRESSIONS

Here are some basic expressions which might come in handy before you set about learning "just enough" Italian:

sì [see]	yes
no [no]	no
grazie [grah-tse'ay]	thank you
prego [preh-go]	you're welcome
per favore [pairr fah-vor-ray]	please
scusi [skoo-zee]	excuse me/sorry

And here are some very useful expressions:

Non capisco [non kah-pees-ko]
   I don't understand
Non parlo (ancora) Italiano
   [non pahr-lo ahn-kor-ah ee-tahl-ee-ah-no]
   I don't speak Italian (yet)
Può parlare più lentamente?
   [poo-o pah-lah-reh pee-oo len-tah-men-teh]
   Could you speak more slowly?

The following are the most frequently-used greetings:

buongiorno [boo'on-jorr-no]	good day
	(used up to mid-afternoon)
buonasera [boo'on-ah-seh-rah]	good evening
buonanotte [boo'on-ah-not-teh]	good night
arrivederci [ahr-ree-veh-dehr-chee]	goodbye

Both **buongiorno** and **buonasera** are used to say "hello" and "goodbye" (depending, of course, on the time of day); **arrivederci** can be used for "goodbye" at any time of day or night, while **buonanotte** is used only on parting at night-time.

   All these are formal greetings, the informal one being the somewhat universal **ciao** [chow], used both to say "hello" and "goodbye", at any time of the day, but only with family, friends and children.

Buongiorno, buonasera, buonanotte and **arrivederci** are often accompanied by the title and/or name of the person you are greeting.

Signore [see-n'yor-reh] is equivalent to "sir" and is used with much the same frequency. It is more commonly used as "Mr.", followed by the surname; in this case it is shortened to **signor** [see-n'yorr].

Signora [see-n'yor-rah], meaning "madam" and (if followed by the surname) "Mrs.", and **signorina** [see-n'yor-ree-nah] "Miss", are used more frequently than their English counterparts.

DAYS OF THE WEEK

il lunedì	Monday
il martedì	Tuesday
il mercoledì	Wednesday
il giovedì	Thursday
il venerdì	Friday
il sabato	Saturday
la domenica	Sunday

MONTHS

gennaio	January
febbraio	February
marzo	March
aprile	April
maggio	May
giugno	June
luglio	July
agosto	August
settembre	September
ottobre	October
novembre	November
dicembre	December

Note that days and months are written without a capital letter.

SEASONS

l'inverno	winter
la primavera	spring
l'estate	summer
l'autunno	autumn

2 Ordering Drinks

There will be many occasions for you to enjoy breakfast, an aperitif or just a drink or snack in an Italian bar. This chapter will help you get yourself a drink.

To order a drink at the counter just name what you want and add **per favore** ('please').

GETTING A COFFEE

Sig. (Mr.) Costa: Un caffè, per favore.
A coffee, please.

Barmaid: Subito.
Straightaway.

Mark: Un caffè macchiato e un cappuccino, per favore.
A white coffee and a cappuccino, please.

Barmaid: Ecco a lei.
Here it is.

Mark: Quant'è?
How much is it?

Barmaid: Tremila.
Three thousand.

IMITATED PRONUNCIATION

Oon kahf-fay, pairr fah-vor-ray.
Soo-be-to.
Oon kahf-fay mah-ke-ah-to eh oon kah-poo-chee-no,
    pairr fah-vor-ray.
Ek-ko.
Kwahn-tay?
Treh-mee-lah.

HOW TO... order a coffee
Un caffè, per favore

ask how much is it
Quant'è?

---

1. A LITTLE PRACTICE

a. Re-read the first two conversations and then order something from the list of drinks below.

b. Ask how much it is.

un caffè* espresso (strong, black coffee)
un caffè macchiato (coffee with a dash of milk)

un cappuccino (coffee with steamed, frothy milk)

un tè al limone (lemon tea)
un tè al latte (tea with milk)

una cioccolata calda (hot chocolate)

* "un caffè" usually means an **espresso**

THE RECEIPT

Later that day Sig. Costa goes for another coffee at a different bar, where the barmaid (**la barista**) tells him that he has to pay beforehand and get a receipt at the cash desk:

Sig. Costa:	Un espresso, per favore.
	An espresso coffee, please.
Barmaid:	Prima deve fare lo scontrino alla cassa.
	You must get the receipt at the cash desk first.

```
        BAR "AL CAMINETTO"
          VIA BELLUNO 18
        TAI DI CADORE (BL)
         P. IVA 00051640258

    BAR           1.800   D4
    DOLCI         1.000   D2
    PANINI        2.500   D1
    BAR           2.200   D4
    000     4     7.500   TL

    CL      8           15-08-93

        PF  AV 43008406
```

After paying at the cash desk, Sig. Costa can order his drink from the barmaid, showing her his receipt.

Sig. Costa:	Un espresso, per favore. Ecco lo scontrino.
	An espresso coffee, please. Here is the receipt.

IMITATED PRONUNCIATION

Oon kahf-fay es-press-so, pairr fah-vor-ray.
Pree-mah deh-veh fah-ray lo skon-tree-no ahl-lah kahs-sah.
Oon es-press-so, pairr fah-vor-ray. Ek-ko lo skon-tree-no.

A LITTLE PRACTICE

a. Re-read the conversation and order a coffee and a snack from the list below.

una brioche	a croissant
una pasta	a bun
un tramezzino	a sandwich
un panino	a filled roll
una focaccia	a piece of filled savoury bread
una pizzetta	a small pizza
un toast	a toasted sandwich
un gelato	an ice cream

"**Cappuccino e brioche**" is a typical Italian bar-breakfast.

AN APERITIF?

Waiter: Cosa prendete?
What would you like?

Mrs. Robins: Un bicchiere di vino bianco e un martini, per favore.
A glass of white wine and a martini, please.

Marco: Cosa prendi, Marisa?
What will you have, Marisa?

Marisa: Un bitter.
A bitter.

Marco: E tu Paolo?
And you, Paolo?

Paolo: Una birra.
A beer.

Marco: Allora un bitter, una birra e un'acqua tonica. Qualcosa da mangiare?
OK, a bitter, a beer and a tonic water. Anything to eat?

Marisa: Ah, sì. Un tramezzino, per favore.
Oh, yes. A sandwich, please.

IMITATED PRONUNCIATION

Ko-sah pren-deh-teh?
Oon beek-yair-eh de vee-no be'ahn-ko eh oon mar-tee-nee, pairr fah-vor-ray.
Ko-sah pren-dee, mah-ree-sah?
Oon bitter.
Eh too, pow'oh-lo?
Oo-nah beer-rah.
Ahl-lor-rah oon bitter, oo-nah beer-rah eh oon-ak-wah ton-ee-kah. Kwahl-ko-sah dah man-jar-ray?
Ah, see. Oon trah-med-zee-no, pairr fah-vor-ray.

HOW TO . . .   Ask "What will you have?"
cosa prendi? (informal)
cosa prende? (formal)
cosa prendete? (plural)

B. A LITTLE PRACTICE

a. Order two items from the list of drinks below.

b. Ask a friend what she/he will have and then order for both of you.

un'acqua minerale gassata	a fizzy mineral water
un'acqua minerale naturale	a still mineral water
un tè freddo	an iced tea
un succo di frutta	a fruit juice
un succo di pera	a pear juice
un succo di albicocca	an apricot juice
una spremuta di arancia	an orange juice
una spremuta di pompelmo	a grapefruit juice
una coca-cola	a coke
un'aranciata	an orangeade
un'acqua tonica	a tonic water
un bicchiere di vino rosso	a glass of red wine
un bicchiere di vino bianco	a glass of white wine
un bitter	a type of aperitif
un martini	a martini
una birra	a beer

Note that for lemom, grapefruit and orange juice, both "**succo**" and "**spremuta**" can be used.

STREETWISE

Bars are a kind of institution in Italy.

Italians often go to the bar at any time of the day – for a quick breakfast on the way to work, for an aperitif before meals and a pick-me-up coffee afterwards, or a snack and a chat whenever they feel like it.

In a bar you can, of course, buy **espresso** and **cappuccino** as well as alcoholic drinks, which are sold throughout the day, and soft drinks and savoury or sweet snacks. Most bars are open from early morning until late at night and some all night.

Sometimes, you may have to pay in advance at the cash desk where you will be given **lo scontrino** (the receipt), to show the barman when you order your drinks.

You can eat and drink standing at the counter (**al banco**), or at one of the tables (**al tavolino**), where you will usually be served by a waiter (**un cameriere**) and pay a little extra for the service.

The list of prices, **il listino prezzi**, will be clearly displayed at the cash desk or counter.

LANGUAGE NOTES

MASCULINE AND FEMININE

In Italian nouns (words for a person, thing or place) are either masculine or feminine. Most nouns ending in **-o** are masculine and most words ending in **-a** are feminine. Be careful though, because this is not always true: **mano**, for example, ends in **-o** but is feminine. Besides, there are also nouns ending in **-e** which can be masculine or feminine: **cane** (dog) is masculine, while **neve** (snow) is feminine.

As you can see, it is not always possible to tell whether a word is masculine or feminine by its ending. You should therefore learn each word with its gender as you go along.

WAYS OF SAYING "A/AN"

In Italian, unlike in English, the gender of nouns affects words like "the" and "a/an", called articles.

For "a" or "an" it's quite simple:

Generally "a" is **un** with a masculine noun and **una** with a feminine one.

But, with masculine nouns beginning with s followed by another consonant, or beginning with z, "a" = **uno**.

And, with feminine nouns beginning with a vowel, "an" = **un'**.

un	**caffè**	a coffee
uno	**scontrino**	a receipt
una	**birra**	a beer
un'	**aranciata**	an orange squash

"The" also takes different forms depending on the gender (masculine or feminine) and number (singular or plural) of the noun, and on the letter with which this begins. Let's look at the singular form first:

Generally "the" = **il** with masculine nouns and **la** with feminine nouns.

But, with masculine nouns beginning with s followed by another consonant, or beginning with z, "the" = **lo,** and with masculine nouns beginning with a vowels (a, e, i, o, u) "the" = **l'**.

The latter also applies to feminine nouns beginning with a vowel: "the" = **l'**.

Now let's look at "the" in the plural. Masculine nouns that have **il** in the singular change this for **i**, and those that have **lo** or **l'** in the singular become **gli**.

All plural feminine nouns, even those beginning with a vowel, have **le** for "the".

Set out as a table, the pattern is like this:

	singular	plural
	singular	plural
masc.	**il** treno (the train)	**i** treni (the trains)
fem.	**la** casa (the house)	**le** case (the houses)
masc.	**lo** zucchero (the sugar)	**gli** zuccheri
masc.	**lo** scontrino (the receipt)	**gli** scontrini
masc.	**l'**aéreo (the plane)	**gli** aerei
fem.	**l'**arancia (the orange)	**le** arancie

How to form the plural of nouns will be explained in the next chapter.

Note that whenever we present you with a new word, its appropriate article will be provided (either at the point of introduction or in the Mini-Dictionary at the end of the book). When you come across a new word, try to memorize it with its article.

NUMBERS FROM 0 TO 10

1	uno	6	sei
2	due	7	sette
3	tre	8	otto
4	quattro	9	nove
5	cinque	10	dieci

NUMBERS FROM 11 ONWARDS

11	undici	20	venti
12	dodici	30	trenta
13	tredici	40	quaranta
14	quattordici	50	cinquanta
15	quindici	60	sessanta
16	sedici	70	settanta
17	diciassette	80	ottanta
18	diciotto	90	novanta
19	diciannove	100	cento

101	centouno
102	centodue
110	centodieci
150	centocinquanta
250	duecentocinquanta
500	cinquecento
1,000	mille
1,500	millecinquecento
2,400	duemilaquattrocento
10,000	diecimila
12,850	dodicimilaottocentocinquanta
45,000	quarantacinquemila
72,650	settantaduemilaseicentocinquanta
125,900	centoventicinquemilanovecento
1,000,000	un milione

2.1
a. Marco is very thirsty. What do you think he would like to order?
i)   un tramezzino
ii) un'aranciata
iii) un caffè

b. Sig. Costa is peckish. What will he have?
i)   un panino
ii) una birra
iii) un tè

c. Marisa is cold and would like a hot drink. What would you order for her?
i)   un tè freddo
ii) una cioccolata
iii) un gelato

2.2
Re-read the lists of drinks and snacks given for the practice exercise on page 21 and complete the following dialogue, ordering something to drink.
Barman: Cosa prende?
You: . . .
Barman: Gassata o naturale?
You: . . .
Barman: Ottocento lire.

VOCABULARY

un caffè, per favore	a coffee, please
il/la barista	the barman/barmaid
Quant'è?	How much is it?
lo scontrino	the receipt
la cassa	the cash desk

Cosa prendi? (*informal*)
Cosa prende? (*formal*) } What will you have?
Cosa prendete? (*plural*)

3 Finding Accommodation

One of the first things you'll need to do when you arrive in Italy is to find somewhere to stay. The following dialogues and notes will tell you how to ask for a room in a hotel, guesthouse or youth hostel, or for a place on a camp site, and enquire about facilities and prices.

A SINGLE ROOM FOR THE NIGHT

Sig. Poli: Buonasera. Avete una camera libera per stanotte?
Good evening. Do you have a vacant room for tonight?

Receptionist: Abbiamo una singola con doccia.
We have a single with shower.

Sig. Poli: Quanto costa?
How much is it?

Receptionist: Quarantamila lire a notte. La prima colazione è compresa.
Forty thousand lire per night. Breakfast is included.

Sig. Poli:	Va bene, la prendo.
	That's fine, I'll take it.
Receptionist:	Mi dà un documento, per favore?
	Can I have your documents, please?
Sig. Poli:	Ecco la mia carta d'identità.
	Here is my identity card.
Receptionist:	Questa è la chiave. Camera diciotta, al secondo piano, sulla destra.
	Here is the key. Room 18, second floor, on the right.

IMITATED PRONUNCIATION

Boo'on-ah-seh-rah. Ah-vay-teh oo-nah kah-mair-rah lee-beh-rah pairr stah-not-teh?

Ahb-yah-mo oo-nah seen-go-lah kon dotch-ah.

Kwahn-to kos-tah?

Kwah-rahn-tah meel-ah leer-reh ah not-teh. Lah pree-mah ko-lah-tse'o-nay eh kom-preh-zah.

Vah beh-neh, lah pren-do.

Me dah oon dok-oo-men-to, pairr fah-vor-ray?

Ek-ko lah mee-ah kahrr-tah dee-dent-ee-tah.

Kwes-tah eh lah kee'ah-vay. Kah-mair-rah dee-chot-to ahl sek-on-do pee'ah-no, sool-lah des-trah.

HOW TO ...   ask for a single/double room with shower
Vorrei una camera singola/doppia con doccia

ask for a double room with bathroom
Vorrei una camera matrimoniale* con bagno

ask how much is the room per night
Quanto costa per notte?

ask if breakfast is included
La colazione è compresa?

ask if you can see the room
È possibile vedere la camera?

* Traditionally, a double bed is **un letto matrimoniale**, hence this alternative term for a double room.

. A LITTLE PRACTICE

a. You are at the reception desk of "Albergo Roma". Ask if they have a single room with bathroom (**con bagno**).

b. Now ask how much it is.

c. How would you ask to see the room?

BOOKING A ROOM BY PHONE

Receptionist: Hotel Granduca, buongiorno.
Granduca Hotel, good afternoon.

Delia: Buongiorno, vorrei prenotare una camera per giovedì notte, per favore.
Good afternoon, I'd like to book a room for Thursday night, please.

Receptionist: Singola o doppia?
Single or double?

Delia: Una doppia. Quanto costa?
A double. How much is that?

Receptionist: Settantamila lire a notte, prima colazione compresa.
Seventy thousand liras per night, with breakfast included.

Delia: Sì, va bene.
That's fine.

Receptionist: Allora una doppia, con doccia, per giovedì 18 (diciotto). Che nome?
So, a double with shower, for Thursday 18th. What name?

Delia: Gardini. G-A-R-D-I-N-I

IITATED PRONUNCIATION

O-tel gran-doo-kah, boo'on-jorr-no.

Boo'on-jorr-no, vor-ray'ee preh-no-tah-reh oo-nah
kah-mair-rah pairr je'o-veh-dee not-teh, pairr fah-vor-ray.

Seen-go-lah oh dop-pe'ah?

Oo-nah dop-pe'ah. Kwahn-to kos-tah?

Set-tahn-tah meel-ah leer-reh ah not-teh, pree-mah
ko-lah-tse'o-nay kom-preh-zah.

See, vah beh-neh.

Ahl-lor-rah oo-nah dop-pe'ah, con dotch-ah, pairr je'o-veh-dee
dee-chot-to. Keh no-may?

Gar-dee-nee. Jee ah ehr-ray dee ee ehn-nay ee.

CHECKING OUT

Sig. Poli: Partirò domani. Mi può preparare il conto, per favore?
I will be leaving tomorrow. Can you prepare my bill, please?

Receptionist: Certamente.
Certainly.

Sig. Poli: Posso pagare con la carta di credito?
Can I pay by credit card?

Receptionist: Certo.
Of course.

Sig. Poli: A che ora devo lasciare la camera?
By what time will I have to leave the room?

Receptionist: Entro mezzogiorno.
By midday.

IMITATED PRONUNCIATION

Pah-teer-ro dom-ah-nee. Mee poo-o pray-pah-rah-ray eel kon-to, pairr fah-vor-ray?
Chairr-tah-men-teh.
Pos-so pah-gah-rray kon lah kahr-tah dee kray-de-to?
Chairr-to.
Ah keh o-rah deh-vo lah-she'ah-ray lah kah-mair-rah?
En-tro med-dzo jorr-no.

30

YOUTH HOSTELS

Claudia: Buonasera. Siamo in quattro, due ragazzi e due ragazze. Avete posto per stanotte?
Good evening. We are four, two guys and two girls. Have you got room for us for tonight?

Clerk: Sì. Mi date i vostri documenti?
Yes. Can I have your documents?

Claudia: Ecco i passaporti. E per mangiare?
Here are our passports. And what about meals?

Clerk: C'è una cucina comune.
There is a communal kitchen.

Claudia: A che ora bisogna rientrare la sera?
What time must we be back by?

Clerk: Chiudiamo a mezzanotte.
We lock the door at midnight.

IMITATED PRONUNCIATION

Boo'o-nah-seh-rah. See'ah-mo in kwaht-tro, doo-ay rah-gaht-see eh doo-ay rah-gaht-seh. Ah-vay-teh pos-to pairr stah-not-teh?
See. Me dah-teh ee vos-tree dok-oo-men-tee?
Ek-ko ee pah-sah-por-tee. Eh pairr mahn-jar-ray?
Chay oo-nah koo-chee-nah kom-moo-neh.
Ah kay o-rah be-son'yah re-en-trah-ray lah seh-rah?
Kee'oo-de-ah-mo ah med-dzah-not-tay.

OW TO... ask if there is room for four
C'è posto per quattro?

ask by what time you have to be back at the hostel at night
A che ora bisogna rientrare la sera?

5. A LITTLE PRACTICE

a. You want to spend the night at an **Ostello della gioventù** (a youth hostel). Ask if there's enough room for you (a girl), your friend and her brother. Remember that you will have to state the sex of your friends.

b. How would you ask at what time they lock up?

 ## CAMPING

Tricia: Buongiorno. Siamo in due, abbiamo la macchina e una tenda. Avete posto?
Good morning. We are two, we have a car and a tent. Have you got room?

Receptionist: Sì, un posto all'ombra.
Yes, a place in the shade.

Tricia: Quanto costa per una settimana?
How much is it for a week?

Receptionist: Centottantamila lire, si paga anticipato. Abbiamo acqua potabile, elettricità, gabinetti, docce. Ci sono anche un mini-market e un bar con telefono pubblico.
One hundred and eighty thousand lire, paid in advance. We have all the facilities – drinking water, electricity, toilets, showers – and also a mini-market and a bar with a public phone.

IMITATED PRONUNCIATION

Boo'on-jorr-no. Se'ah-mo on doo-ay, ahb-yah-mo lah mahk-e-nah eh oo-nah ten-dah. Ah-vay-teh pos-to?

See, oon pos-to ahl-lom-brah.

Kwahn-to kos-tah pairr oo-nah sett-ee-mah-nah?

Chent-ot-tan-tah meel-ah leer-reh, see pah-gah ahn-titchy-pah-to. Ahb-yah-mo ak-wah pot-ah-be-leh, eh-leh-tre-se-tah, gah-be-net-tee, dotch-ay. Chee so-no ahn-keh oon mini-market eh oon bar kon teh-lay-fo-no poob-le-ko.

6. A LITTLE PRACTICE

a. You have just arrived at the camp site "**Camping Miramare**". Ask if there is room for your family of three with one car and a tent.

b. Now ask how much it is per day.

 PROBLEMS WITH THE HOT WATER

Matthew:	Scusi, volevo fare una doccia, ma non c'è acqua calda.
	Excuse me, I wanted to take a shower, but there isn't any hot water.
Receptionist:	Ha lasciato scorrere l'acqua per un po'?
	Did you let the water run for a bit?
Matthew:	Sì.
	Yes.
Receptionist:	Mmm, potrebbe essere la caldaia. Vado a vedere.
	Mmm, it could be the boiler. I'll go and have a look.

IMITATED PRONUNCIATION

Skoo-ze, vo-lay-vo fah-reh oo-nah dotch-yah, mah non chay ahk-wah kahl-dah.

Ah lah-she'ah-to skor-rair-reh lahk-wah pairr oon po?

See.

Mmm, pot-reb-beh ess-air-eh lah kahl-dah-e'ah. Vah-do ah veh-day-reh.

That, incidentally, will be the last dialogue for which we give you the imitated pronunciation. By now you should have grasped the basics and be getting quite good at making the right sounds; if you still find pronunciation difficult, and you haven't bought the cassettes because you didn't think they'd be necessary, then we recommend them now.

You can find somewhere to stay in an **albergo** or a **hotel**, classified according to the international star code or divided into **categorie** (categories): **di lusso** (deluxe), **prima** (first), **seconda** (second), **terza** (third)

A **pensione** is a family-run hotel, a sort of guesthouse. It may offer fewer services than hotels, but, on the other hand, be friendlier and cheaper. Breakfast is always provided.

The price of the room will not necessarily include breakfast. You will have to ask "**la colazione è compresa?**". It might be possible to have half board (breakfast and evening meal at the hotel or pension), and you will have to state "**mezza pensione**" or, for full board (breakfast, lunch and evening meal) "**pensione completa**".

It is always a good idea to book in advance, especially in the high season. You can do this directly or through special agencies (the Italian Tourist Office will supply you with their telephone numbers). If you arrive in a big town, you can ask for information at the Tourist Information Office, **l'Azienda d Soggiorno e Turismo**.

camera singola	single room
camera matrimoniale	room with double bed
camera doppia	twin room
con bagno	with bathroom
con doccia	with shower
senza bagno	the bathroom is not en-suite

Cheaper accommodation can be found in an **Ostello della gioventù**, a youth hostel. Although most popular with young people, there are no age limits. Remember that usually you can't check in until late afternoon and you may have to respect a "curfew".

Camping may be another holiday option. There are many camp sites, **campeggi**, in Italy. You are always advised to camp on official sites, lists of which can be obtained from the Italian Tourist Office.

camping	camp site
camping vietato	no camping
proprietà privata	private property

LANGUAGE NOTES

PLURALS

In English it is very easy to make the plural of a noun: usually you just add an "-s" to the end of the word. Generally in Italian, words ending in **-a** have their plural ending in **-e**, if they are feminine:

la ragazza (the girl)　　　　　**le ragazze** (the girls)

and in **-i** if they are masculine:

il turista (the tourist)　　　　　**i turisti** (the tourist)

Words ending in **-o** or in **-e** have their plural ending in **-i**:

un ragazzo (a boy)　　　　　**due ragazzi** (two boys)
la pensione (the guesthouse)　**le pensioni** (the guesthouses)

Some words are invariable, with the plural form the same as the singular:

la città (the town)　　　　　**le città** (the towns)
lo sci (the ski)　　　　　　　**gli sci** (the skis)
il bar (the bar)　　　　　　　**i bar** (the bars)

This usually happens when the word ends with an accented vowel, "i", or a consonant.

SOME USES OF "FOR", "WITH", "WITHOUT"

per = for
per stanotte = for tonight
per una settimana = for a week
per il bambino = for the child

con = **with**
con bagno/doccia = with bath/shower
con latte = with milk

senza = **without**
senza bagno = without bathroom
senza zucchero = without sugar

YOUR TURN

3.1

Try to match the following symbols with the right explanation:
a) camera singola con bagno
b) camera doppia con doccia
b) camera matrimoniale senza bagno

1)   2)   3)

 3.2

Listen to the tape. The gentleman talking is booking a room.
Listen carefully and say whether of the following statements are
true or false.

	VERO true	FALSO false
a) He wants a double room.		
b) With en-suite bathroom.		
c) He will stay three days.		
d) He will pay cash.		

 3.3

Mark has just arrived at a youth hostel, with two other friends. He
would like to stay for two nights. Fill in his conversation with the
receptionist (if you don't have the tapes you can still work this
exercise by writing down the answer):

Receptionist: Buonasera.
                  Good evening.
Mark: . . .
Receptionist: Per quanti?
                  For how many?
Mark: . . .
Receptionist: Per quante notti?
                  For how many nights?
Mark: . . .

3.4

Let's see how good you are at translation, putting Italian into English. All the words and sentences have appeared in the text you've read so far, so try not to check back unless you get absolutely stuck!

a) Non c'è acqua calda.

b) Questa è la chiave, camera diciotto.

c) Un posto all'ombra.

d) Mi può preparare il conto, per favore?

e) La (prima) colazione è compresa.

f) Quanto costa per un settimana?

g) Partirò domani.

VOCABULARY

l' albergo	the hotel
la pensione	the guesthouse
Avete una camera libera?	Have you got a room?
una camera singola	a single room
una camera matrimoniale	a double room (with double bed)
una camera doppia	a room with twin beds
con bagno	with bathroom
con doccia	with shower
senza bagno	the bathroom is not en-suite
Vorrei una camera singola con doccia	I would like a single room with shower
Quanto costa?	How much is it?
La prima colazione è compresa?	Is breakfast included?
È possibile vedere la camera?	Is it possible to see the room?
l'ostello della gioventù	the youth hostel
il campeggio/camping	the camp site
camping vietato	no camping
Avete posto per stanotte?	Have you got room for tonight?
Posso pagare con la carta di credito?	Can I pay by credit card?
A che ora devo lasciare la camera?	By what time will I have to leave the room?

4 Meeting People

One thing to remember when meeting people, introducing yourself and generally making conversation, is the level of formality of your relationship with them. The following dialogues present both familiar and more formal language examples.

INTRODUCING YOURSELF

Paola:	Ciao.
	Hi.
Andrew:	Ciao.
	Hi.
Paola:	Come ti chiami?
	What's your name?
Andrew:	Mi chiamo Andrew. E tu, come ti chiami?
	My name's Andrew. And what's yours?
Paola:	Io sono Paola.
	I'm Paola.

Sig. (Mr.) Costa:	Buongiorno.
	Good morning.
Sig. Robins:	Buongiorno.
	Good morning.
Sig. Costa:	Mi chiamo Matteo Costa.
	My name is Matteo Costa.
Sig. Robins:	Io mi chiamo Peter Robins.
	My name is Peter Robins.
Sig. Costa:	Piacere.
	How do you do?
Sig. Robins:	Molto lieto.
	How do you do?

HOW TO... say your name
Mi chiamo Peter Robinson
Mi chiamo Andrew

ask someone's name
Come si chiama? (form.)
Come ti chiami? (inf.)

7. A LITTLE PRACTICE

a. Introduce yourself.
b. Now imagine asking someone his/her name. Remember to use the formula you think is most appropriate (formal or informal).

 ENQUIRING ABOUT SOMEONE'S NATIONALITY

Paola: Sei straniero?
Are you a foreigner?

Andrew: Sì, sono inglese. E tu sei italiana?
Yes, I am English. And are you Italian?

Paola: Sì, io sono italiana.
Yes, I'm Italian

Sig. Costa: Lei è italiano?
Are you Italian?

Sig. Robins: No, sono scozzese. E lei?
No, I'm Scottish. And you?

Sig. Costa: Io sono italiano.
I'm Italian.

HOW TO... ask if someone is Italian
Lei è italiano/a? (form.)
Sei italiano/a? (inf.)

say "yes, I am Italian"
Sì, sono italiano/a

say "no, I am English"
No, sono inglese

8. A LITTLE PRACTICE

a. Memorize the list of nationalities below and then practise saying you are Italian/English etc . . .

italiano/a (Italian)
inglese (English)
scozzese (Scottish)
irlandese (Irish)
gallese (Welsh)
tedesco/a (German)
francese (French)
spagnolo/a (Spanish)
americano/a (American)
australiano/a (Australian)
straniero/a (foreign)

INTRODUCING SOMEONE

Sig. Costa: Signor Robins, le presento Carlo Fabbri.
Mr. Robins, this is Carlo Fabbri.

Sig. Robins: Piacere di conoscerla.
How do you do?

Sig. Fabbri: Piacere mio.
How do you do?

Paola: Andrew, questo è mio fratello Luca.
Andrew, this is my brother Luca.

Andrew: Ciao, Luca.
Hi.

Luca: Ciao.
Hi.

Incidentally, you may have noticed in the dialogue translations that the English doesn't always appear to match up with the Italian (e.g. "How do you do? for "Piacere", "Piacere di conoscerla", and the responses "Piacere mio", "Molto lieto"). Don't worry about these free translations; it's better you should quickly get the gist of what's being said, than learn a literal word-for-word version that may need further explanation.

9. A LITTLE PRACTICE

a. How would you introduce two of your friends to each other?

b. And what about two colleagues?

 ASKING WHERE SOMEONE IS FROM

Sig. Costa:	Di dov'è, signor Robins?
	Where are you from, Mr. Robins?
Sig. Robins:	Sono di Edimburgo. E lei di dov'è?
	I'm from Edinburgh. And where are you from?
Sig. Costa:	Sono di Firenze.
	I'm from Florence.

Andrew:	Di dove sei?
	Where are you from?
Paola:	Sono nata a Pisa, ma abito a Firenze. E tu?
	I was born in Pisa, but I live in Florence. And you?
Andrew:	Sono di Londra.
	I'm from London.

10. A LITTLE PRACTICE
a. Say which town you come from.
b. Now imagine asking someone you have just met where they come from.

STREETWISE

TU/LEI

Whilst in English there is only one form for "you", in Italian there are two ways of addressing people as "you": "**tu**" and "**lei**".

Tu is used with members of one's family, friends and children. It sets the language on an informal level. It requires the 2nd person singular of verbs (usually the second in lists provided in most reference books).

Example: **Tu sei inglese?** Are you English?

Lei is a more formal way of addressing people and therefore used with people you don't know or with whom you are on formal terms. It requires the 3rd person singular of verbs (the third in the list):

Example: **Lei è inglese?** Are you English?

Lei, meaning "you", is used for male and female, but it also means "she":

Example: **Lei è inglese?** Is she English?

If you are a man, be careful, then – if someone is addressing you as "**lei**", don't turn around thinking they are talking to a woman instead of you!

dare del lei = to address formally
dare del tu = to address informally, to be on first-name terms

When talking to someone you have recently met, it is quite common to be told **diamoci del tu**. If you want to be more informal with that person, then you can swap from **lei** to the easier form **tu**.

SHAKING HANDS

Italians do shake hands, but not all the time. They do so when introduced to someone for the first time, and when they meet again or say goodbye to someone they know on formal terms.

With family and close friends the greetings are often accompanied by kisses, one on each cheek, if they have not seen each other for a while.

LANGUAGE NOTES

I, YOU, HE/SHE, WE, THEY

io	I
tu	you (familiar, singular)
lui	he
lei	she
lei	you (formal, singular)
noi	we
voi	you (plural)
loro	they

In Italian it is not always necessary to use these words (subject personal pronouns), as it is in English. Note that to say "I am Italian" you can say "**Sono italiano**", that is you don't have to use the word for "I". But you can also say "**Io sono italiano**" (or, if you're a woman, "**Io sono italiana**" – as you'll learn in the next section).

ADJECTIVES

Italian adjectives (words describing qualities,nationalities etc.), agree in gender and number with the person or thing to which they are referring. So you have:

Paola è simpatica (Paola is friendly)
Andrew è simpatico (Andrew is friendly)
Il signor Costa è italiano (Mr. Costa is Italian)
Paola è italiana (Paola is Italian)

With adjectives ending in **-e** there is no such distinction:
Andrew è inglese **Lisa è inglese**

YOUR TURN

4.1
Fill in the dialogue. You can write down your part and then compare it with the key at the back of the book. Practise saying your part out loud, which will be more fun if you have the tapes, as the other parts of the conversation are recorded.

– . . . ? [What's your name?]

– Mi chiamo Matthew

– . . . ? [Are you English?]

– No, sono americano. E tu?

– . . . [I'm Italian.]

– . . . ? [[Where are you from?]

– Sono di Roma.

4.2
You've done one exercise translating from Italian into English; now try it the other way round:
a) Are you (formal) Scots?
b) I live in Edinburgh.
c) She is English, and friendly.
d) You (familiar) are from London.
e) This is my brother Andrew. (an informal introduction)

VOCABULARY

ciao	hi/hello/bye
mi chiamo . . .	my name is . . .
Io sono . . .	I'm . . .
buongiorno	good morning
Piacere	How do you do?
Come ti chiami?	What's your name? (informal)
Come si chiama?	What's your name? (formal)
Sei inglese?	Are you English? (informal)
È inglese?	Are you English? (formal)
Sei italiano/a?	Are you Italian? (informal)
È italiano/a?	Are you Italian? (formal)
Sono inglese	I am English
Sono italiano/a	I am Italian
Questo è . . .	This is . . . (when introducing someone informally)
Le presento . . .	This is . . . (formal introduction)
Di dove sei?	Where are you from? (informal)
Di dov'è?	Where are you from? (formal)
Sono di . . .	I am from . . .
Come stai?	How are you? (informal)
Come sta?	How are you? (formal)

5 Around Town

Today it is Andrew's first day in Pisa. He decides to buy a map of the town and asks a passer-by where the nearest newsagent is.

WHERE IS . . . ?

Andrew: Scusi, c'è un giornalaio qui vicino?
Excuse me, is there a newsagent nearby?

Passer-by: Sì, in Piazza Matteotti.
Yes, in Piazza Matteotti.

Andrew: Dov'è?
Where is that?

Passer-by: Prende la prima strada a sinistra e arriva in una piazzetta. Il giornalaio è sulla destra, accanto alla farmacia.
Take the first road on the left and you come to a small square. The newsagent is on the right, next to the chemist's.

Andrew: Grazie.
Thank you.

HOW DO I . . . ?

Andrew wants to visit the town. His first stop is, of course, the leaning Tower. He asks a passer-by (**un passante**) for directions.

Andrew: Scusi, per andare alla Torre?
Excuse me, how do I get to the Tower?

Passante: È in Piazza dei Miracoli. Attraversa il ponte e al semaforo gira a destra. Poi prende la prima a sinistra e continua sempre dritto. Si troverà la torre davanti.
It's in Piazza dei Miracoli. Cross the bridge and turn right at the traffic light. Then take the first on the left and keep going straight on. You will see the Tower in front of you.

Andrew: È lontano a piedi?
Is it far on foot?

Passante: No, dieci minuti.
No, ten minutes.

Andrew: Grazie. Arrivederci.
Thank you. Goodbye.

Passante: Prego.
You are welcome.

HOW TO... ask how to get to the tower
Scusi, per andare alla Torre?

ask if it is far (on foot)
È lontano (a piedi)?

1. A LITTLE PRACTICE

a. Read the first two dialogues again and ask where the following places are:

l'Ente del turismo (the tourist office)
la stazione (the railway station)
il duomo (the Cathedral)

 IS THERE . . . ?

Mrs. Robins needs to find a phone. She asks a traffic warden (**un vigile urbano**) where to find one.

Mrs. Robins: Scusi, dov'è un telefono pubblico?
Excuse me, where is there a public phone?

Traffic warden: Ce n'è uno in Via Crispi, a cinque minuti da qui.
There is one in via Crispi, five minutes from here.

Mrs. Robins: Come ci si arriva?
How do I get there?

Traffic warden: Continua a dritto per questa strada e all'incrocio gira a sinistra . . .
Go straight along this road and at the junction turn left . . .

Mrs. Robins: All'incrocio giro a sinistra.
At the junction turn left.

Traffic warden: Sì. Subito dietro l'angolo c'è una cabina telefonica.
Yes. Just around the corner there is a telephone box.

Mrs. Robins: Grazie tante.
Thank you very much.

2. A LITTLE PRACTICE

a. How would you ask how to get to the British Consulate (**il Consolato Britannico**)?

MAPS

Maps can be bought at most bookshops, tobacconists and newsagents or are available free at tourist offices. For a town plan, ask for **una piantina della città.**

ASKING THE WAY

Remember that in Italy, an address is given with the house number coming after the street name (**Via dei Pecori 57**). It's a good idea to write down the address you're looking for, before you ask how to find it. When you're given directions, which will doubtless be accompanied by various hand signals and arm-waving, try to slow the speaker down (say **Per favore, parli più lentamente**, "Please speak more slowly", or **Come?** "Pardon?"), and repeat the main elements of his or her instructions. The important words to listen out for are:

passi per . . .	go along . . .
giri . . . **/gira** . . .	turn . . .
vada . . .	go . . .
vada oltre . . .	go past the . . .
prenda . . .	take . . .
(gira) a destra	(turn) right
(gira) a sinistra	(turn) left
dritto/sempre dritto	straight on
il primo a/la prima a . . .	first on the . . .
il secondo a/la seconda a . . .	second on the . . .

If you really can't make head or tail of what you hear (the speaker may have a thick regional accent, after all), you could ask him or her to write down the directions – **Me lo scriva, p favore**) – it might help.

LANGUAGE NOTES

WHERE IS/ARE . . . ?

"Where" is **dove**; to ask "Where is the station?" you say **Dov'è la stazione?** Notice that **dove** is shortened to **dov'** when coming before **è** ("is"), and that the stress shifts to the second syllable . . . *dóh-veh* becomes *doh-véh*.

"Where are . . . ?" is **dove sono?** For example: **Dove sono le sue valigie?** = Where are your suitcases?

HERE IS/ARE

The same form of abbreviation happens to **ce**, "there": when it comes before **è** to mean "there is", you get **c'è**:
C'è un bar qui vicino = There is a bar nearby.

If followed by a question mark or pronounced with rising intonation, it means "is there . . . ?":
C'è un bar qui vicino? = Is there a bar nearby?

The answer to this question might well be:
Ce n'è uno in piazza = There is one in the square.
The **n** appears before the verb (**è**) to refer to "one of them"; you use it in order to avoid repeating "**bar**".

Ci sono is the plural form ("there are . . . "), and it can be turned into a question ("are there . . . ?) the same way:
Ci sono molti musei? = Are there many museums?
Non ci sono molti turisti = There aren't many tourists

5.1

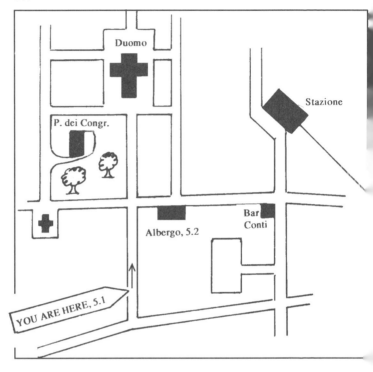

Follow the directions below. Where are you going?

Prende la prima a destra, prosegue dritto fino al Bar Conti, poi gira a sinistra.

a) al duomo
b) alla stazione
c) al Bar Conti

5.2

Mrs. Robins needs to go to the Conference Hall. She asks the hotel receptionist for directions. Look at the map on the previous page and complete the dialogue.

Mrs. Robins: . . . Palazzo dei Congressi?

Receptionist: Quando esce dall'albergo gira a sinistra e va sempre dritto fino alla chiesa. Sulla destra c'è un parco e il Palazzo dei Congressi è lì dentro.

Mrs. Robins: . . . ?

Receptionist: No, dieci minuti a piedi.

Mrs. Robins: . . .

Receptionist: Prego.

VOCABULARY

la piantina della città	town map
la fermata dell'autobus	bus stop
c'è un/una . . . ?	is there a . . . ?
qui vicino	nearby
dov'è . . . ?	where is . . . ?
è lontano?	is it far?
di fronte a . . .	in front of . . .
accanto a . . .	next to . . .
vicino a . . .	near
prenda	take
gira a destra/sinistra	turn left/right
sempre dritto	straight on
il semaforo	traffic light
l'incrocio	crossroads, junction

6 Travelling Around!

In this chapter you will find out how to buy a travel ticket, enquire about prices and timetables, and how to hire a car.

Andrew wants to go to via Santa Maria. He needs to catch the bus and enquires at the bus information booth, where he also buys his tickets.

BY BUS

Andrew: Scusi, qual è l'autobus per Via Santa Maria?
Excuse me, which is the bus to Via Santa Maria?

Clerk: Il numero dodici.
Number 12.

Andrew: Mi dà due biglietti, per favore?
Two tickets, please.

Clerk: Millesettecento.
One thousand seven hundred (lire).

Andrew: Dove devo scendere?
Where do I get off?

Clerk: Alla quinta fermata. Può chiedere all'autista di dirle quando scendere.
At the fifth stop. You can ask the driver to tell you when to get off.

Andrew: Dov'è la fermata?
Where is the bus stop?

Clerk: È qui a destra.
It's here on the right.

Andrew: Grazie.
Thank you.

13. A LITTLE PRACTICE

a. You want to go to the station. How would you ask which bus to take?

b. And what would you say to ask where to get off?

 BY TAXI

Mrs. Robins is going back to her hotel by taxi. Here is her conversation with the taxi driver (**il tassista**).

Mrs. Robins: Albergo Granduca, in Via San Martino, per favore.
Can you take me to the Granduca Hotel, Via San Martino, please.

Driver: Certamente, signora!
Of course, madam!

Driver: Eccoci.
Here we are.

Mrs. Robins: Quanto le devo?
How much is it?

Driver: Cinquemila lire.
5000 liras.

Mrs. Robins: Mi può fare una ricevuta?
Can you give me a receipt?

Driver: Ecco a lei.
Here you are.

4. A LITTLE PRACTICE

    a. Ask the taxi driver to take you to the station.
    b. How would you ask how much is it to go there?
    c. Ask for a receipt.

 BY TRAIN

Mrs. Robins is buying a ticket to Vicenza. She enquires about the departure time and platform.

Mrs. Robins: Un biglietto per Vicenza, per favore.
                A ticket for Vicenza, please.
      Clerk: Solo andata?
                Single?
Mrs. Robins: No, andata e ritorno, grazie.
                No, return, please.
                A che ora parte il treno?
                When does the train leave?
      Clerk: Alle quindici e cinquanta.
                At three fifty p.m.
Mrs. Robins: Da che binario?
                From which platform?
      Clerk: Dal binario cinque.
                From platform 5.

BY UNDERGROUND

Mrs Robins wants to buy a ticket for the tube. She can't operate the ticket machine so she asks an attendant for help.

Mrs. Robins: Scusi, devo fare il biglietto ma non capisco le istruzioni. Potrebbe aiutarmi, per favore?
Excuse me, I need a ticket but I don't understand the instructions. Can you help me, please?

Attendant: Certo. Dove deve andare?
Sure. Where are you going?

Mrs Robins: In Piazza Sab Babila.
To Piazza San Babila.

Attendant: Allora le serve un biglietto urbano che costa milleduecento lire, vede qui "IMPORTO DA INTRODURRE: LIRE 1200". Ha della moneta? "LA MACCHINA NON DÀ RESTO"
Then you need a "town ticket" which costs 1200 lire, you see here "AMOUNT TO INSERT: 1200 lire". Have you got some change? "THE MACHINE IS EXACT FARE ONLY".

Mrs. Robins: Sì. Che monete prende?
Yes. What coins does it take?

Attendant: "MONETE DA LIRE 100, 200, 500" (cento, duecento, cinquecento).
100, 200, 500 lire coins.

Mrs. Robins: *(Inserts the coins and gets her ticket)*
Grazie tante per il suo aiuto.
Thank you very much for your help.

Attendant: Prego, arrivederci.
You're welcome. Goodbye.

HOW TO... ask for help in buying your ticket from the machine
Scusi, potrebbe aiutarmi a fare il biglietto, per favore?

ask for one single/return ticket to Vicenza
(Un biglietto per) Vicenza solo andata/andata e ritorno

ask at what time the train to Vicenza leaves
A che ora parte il treno per Vicenza?

ask from which platform it leaves
Da che binario?

5. A LITTLE PRACTICE

a. Ask for two single tickets to Rome.
b. How would you ask at what time the train for Rome leaves?
c. And how about from which platform?

ask "What time is it?"
Che ore sono, per favore?
or **Che ora è?**

HIRING A CAR

Mrs. Robins would like to hire a car. She looks up in **le pagine gialle** (yellow pages) and calls AVIS.

Mrs. Robins: Buongiorno, vorrei sapere quanto costa noleggiare una macchina per due giorni, sabato e domenica.
Good morning, I'd like to know how much is it to hire a car for two days, Saturday and Sunday.

Impiegato: Per una Peugeot duecento cinque, una Ypsilon dieci o un'Opel Corsa viene duecentoquarantamila lire tutto compreso: IVA assicurazione, chilometraggio illimitato. Il pagamento è tramite carta di credito.
For a Peugeot 205, an Ypsilon 10 or an Opel Corsa is two hundred and forty thousand liras – VAT, insurance, unlimited mileage included. You pay by credit card.

Mrs. Robins: Vorrei prenotare, allora.
Fine, I'd like to book.

Impiegata: Quando viene a ritirare la macchina deve portare la patente e un documento. Mi dà i suo dati per favore . . .
When you come to collect the car, you must bring your driving licence and some other proof of identit Can I have your details please . . . ?

HOW TO... say you would like to hire a car.
Vorrei prenotare una macchina.

ask if they can deliver the car to your hotel.
Potete portarla al mio albergo?

---

16. A LITTLE PRACTICE

a. Ask how much it is to hire a car for a week.
b. How would you ask if the insurance is included?

In most towns buses are bright orange. In some towns you can still find trams.

You must buy the ticket (**il biglietto**) before boarding the bus. Tickets are available in tobacconists and newsagents displaying a "**Punto vendita** . . . " sticker and at bus kiosks. When you get on the bus, using the rear or sometimes the front door, marked "**SALITA**" (to get off use the central one marked "**USCITA**"), you must validate the ticket in the machine. You will be fined if an inspector finds you without a ticket or a non-validated one.

Routes and timetables (buses are often not on time, but they are usually quite frequent!) are displayed at most bus-stops (**la fermata**). The bus service generally starts early in the morning and stops around 11 p.m., although it varies from route to route and town to town.

You can buy a flat-rate ticket, valid for one ride only, or a timed-ticket, which is valid for a certain length of time (**biglietto orario**), within which you can use the ticket for as many rides as you want. You can then purchase a monthly pass and, in more touristy towns, a special tourist pass.

Rail travel is quite cheap in Italy, so it is very widely used – which means that during the tourist season you'd be well advised to book your seat in advance. This won't cost you any extra, but you will have to pay a supplement for travelling on an **EC** (Eurocity), **IC** (Intercity) or **rapido** train. The latter is a long-distance, fast service, stopping at main stations. Other types of train are:

locale / regionale: small local train stopping at all stations;
diretto: stops at most stations and thus hardly 'direct'!
espresso: long-distance, stopping at main stations, reasonably fast.

You can buy your train ticket at the station from **la biglietteria** (ticket office), or from the ticket machines if available. Some types of ticket can be bought at travel agents. You cannot buy a ticket on the train, and you'll be charged a penalty fee plus the ticket price if you are caught without one. If you have a return ticket, you should validate it by getting it date-stamped on the day you return. In most stations there are ticket-stamping machines, but in smaller stations you should go to the ticket office.

TAXIS

Italian taxis are usually yellow and are always marked TAXI It's easier to find one in taxi ranks at stations and central squares or by phoning, rather than hailing one in the street. There are supplementary charges for luggage, higher rates on Sundays and public holidays and between 10 p.m. and 7 a.m. Sometimes, especially for a longer journey, it's better to discuss the fare beforehand.

THE UNDERGROUND

The underground system (**la metropolitana** or **metro**) is in Milan, Rome and Naples only. Station entrances are marked with a big M. Underground tickets are the same as those for the bus and can be bought from the machines at main stations as well as from most newsagents and tobacconists. The price is fixed, irrespective of the destination. (The timed ticket can be used for one journey only.)

The underground starts at around 6.00 a.m. and stops at around midnight.

CAR RENTAL

You can find car rental services at airports and major train stations or look in the yellow pages under "**autonoleggio**". To rent a car you must be at least 21 years old and have held a clean driving licence for at least one year.

A few things to remember when in Italy:
– Drive on the right-hand side of the road and give priority to vehicles coming from the right!
– The motorway, "**l'autostrada**", is not free in Italy; you must pay a toll fee (**pedaggio**); however, the **superstrada** is a motorway free of charge.
– You don't help yourself at a petrol station, unless it is self-service. You can ask for "**il pieno**" (full up) or say the amount of money you want to spend, for example "**trentamila, per favore**"; many petrol stations close for lunch, but there are 24-hour self-service ones.
– It is against the law to carry a can of petrol in your car.

benzina normale = 2 star
super = 4 star

LANGUAGE NOTES

ESSERE (TO BE)

io sono	I am
tu sei	you are (informal)
lui è	he is
lei è	she is
lei è	you are (formal)
noi siamo	we are
voi siete	you are (plural)
loro sono	they are

(io) sono inglese	I am English
(tu) sei italiano	you are Italian
Peter è un ingegnere	Peter is an engineer
Paola è un'infermiera	Paola is a nurse
lei è scozzese	you (formal) are Scottish
(noi) siamo di Londra	we are from London
(voi) siete di Roma	you are from Rome
(loro) sono in vacanza	they are on holiday

"THIS AND THAT"

As you may have guessed, "this" and "that" agree with the words they refer to.

"This book" and "this door" will be:

<u>questo</u> libro and <u>questa</u> porta
(<u>questi</u> libri and <u>queste</u> porte for the plural).

"That book" and "that door" will be:

<u>quel</u> libro and <u>quella</u> porta
(<u>quei</u> libri and <u>quelle</u> porte for the plural).

"MY", "YOUR", "HIS/HER", "OUR", "THEIR"

These words, called possessive adjectives ("my" etc) and pronouns ("mine" etc), usually come in front of the noun and are preceded by **il/la** etc. The important thing to remember is that they agree in number and gender with the thing possessed, <u>not</u> with the owner.

Thus, Maria will refer to "my hotel" as **il mio albergo** (of course she doesn't actually have to own it!), while John will say **la mia valigia** - "my suitcase". Both **mio** and **mia** reflect the gender of the nouns to which they refer. Here are some more examples:

il suo albergo (his/her hotel): you use the masculine **suo** because **albergo** is masculine.
la sua valigia (his/her suitcase): you use the feminine **sua** because **valigia** is feminine.
i miei libri (my books): you use the masculine plural **miei** to agree with the gender and number of **libri**.

Each form has four different endings, two for each gender in the singular, and again for the plural. Here's a table:

m.sing.	f.sing.	m.pl.	f.pl	
il mio	la mia	i miei	le mie	my, mine
il tuo	la tua	i tuoi	le tue	your, yours (inf.)
il suo	la sua	i suoi	le sue	his/her(s), your, yours (form.)
il nostro	la nostra	i nostri	le nostre	our, ours
il vostro	la vostra	i vostri	le vostre	your, yours (pl.)
il loro	la loro	i loro	le loro	their, theirs

ELLING THE TIME

We told you how to ask "What time is it?" - **Che ore sono, per favore?** or more simply **Che ora è?** – but you don't know how to answer. Here are a few pointers and basic phrases, and there are some "time" words for you to learn in the following vocabulary section.

The hour is expressed in Italian by the ordinal number only (there's no equivalent of "o'clock"):

Sono le due	It's two o'clock
Sono le tre	It's three o'clock
Sono le quattro	It's four o'clock

Note that "one o'clock" alone is a little different: **è l'una.**

To say "half past", add **e mezzo** after the hour. "Quarter past" is just as simple - add **e un quarto:**

Sono le nove e mezzo	It's half past nine
Sono le nove e un quarto	It's quarter past nine

"Quarter to" an hour can be said in two ways, either by adding **e tre quarti** to the hour, or by adding **meno un quarto** ("less a quarter") to the next hour:

Sono le nove e tre quarti	It's nine forty-five
Sono le dieci meno un quarto	It's quarter to ten

Minutes past the hour are expressed by adding the number of minutes to the current hour number, while for minutes to the hour you add **meno** followed by the number of minutes to the next hour:

Sono le undici e cinque	It's five past eleven
Sono le undici e venti	It's twenty past eleven
Sono le sei meno cinque	It's five to six
Sono le sei meno venti	It's twenty to six

"At two o'clock" is **alle due.** There aren't any "a.m."/"p.m." equivalents in Italian, so if you want to say "at ten a.m." you have to make this "at ten in the morning", **alle le dieci di mattina.** Ten at night is **le dieci di sera** - it's always questionable as to when evening (**sera**) ends and night (**notte**) begins. "2 a.m." could be **le due di notte,** but also **le due del mattino.**

YOUR TURN

6.1
Fill the gaps in the questions and answers with the words below:

a) . . . l'autobus per il centro?   Il . . . 3.

b) **Dov'è . . . ?**   **Di . . . alla banca.**

c) **Qual è . . . per il Duomo?**   **La rossa e . . . gialla.**

d) **Alla Scala, . . . favore?**   **Subito.**

la linea – fronte – la fermata – mi porta – numero – la – qual è – per

6.2
To go from one of Milan's airports "**Aeroporto Malpensa**" to the city centre, you need to get a coach (**il pullman**) to the "**Stazione Centrale**", the central railway station. You are with three friends, what would you say at the ticket office?

VOCABULARY

Qual è l'autobus per . . . ?	Which is the bus to . . . ?
il biglietto	the ticket
Dove devo scendere per . . . ?	Where do I get off for . . . ?
Dov'è la fermata?	Where is the bus stop?
della moneta	some change
la macchinetta	the machine
Quanto le devo?	How much do I owe you?
solo andata	single
andata e ritorno	return
il binario	the platform
un posto	a seat
noleggiare	to hire
l'assicurazione	the insurance
il chilometraggio	mileage
il pagamento	the payment
la carta di credito	the credit card
la patente	the driving licence
un documento	a document
la stazione centrale	central station
Arrivi	arrivals
Partenze	departures
ai binari	to the platforms
fumatori	smoking
non fumatori	no-smoking
prima/seconda classe	first/second class
la prenotazione	reservation
la riduzione	reduction
la carrozza ristorante	dining car
il vagone letto	sleeping car
la carrozza cuccetta	couchette
un minuto	one minute
dieci minuti	ten minutes
una mezz'ora	half an hour
un'ora	one hour
il giorno	day
la mattina/il mattino	morning
il pomeriggio	afternoon
la sera	evening
la notte	night
ieri	yesterday
oggi	today
domani	tomorrow
dopodomani	the day after tomorrow

7

Out and About

This chapter will show you how to carry out some basic tasks, such as changing money at the bank, buying stamps and postcards, and make a telephone call to Britain.

Mrs. Robins needs to change some pounds into Italian lire. She goes to the bank (**la banca**) at the exchange desk (**l'ufficio cambi**).

AT THE BANK

Mrs. Robins: Buongiorno, vorrei cambiáre delle sterline.
Good morning, I'd like to change some pounds.

Clerk: In lire italiane?
Into Italian lire?

Mrs. Robins: Sì.
Yes.

Clerk: Quante sterline vuole cambiare?
How many pounds would you like to change?

Mrs. Robins: Duecento. Eccole. Quant'è il cambio?
Two hundred. Here it is. What is the exchange rate?

Clerk: Oggi duemilaquattrocentonovanta lire.
Today 2,490 liras.

[*He counts the money*] Cento, duecento, trecento, quattrocento. Cinquanta, sessanta, settanta, ottanta, novanta. Novantacinque, novantasei, novantasette e novantotto.

Quattrocentonovantottomila lire. Ecco a lei.
100, 200, 300, 400. 50, 60, 70, 80, 90. 95, 96, 97 and 98. 498,000 lire. Here you are.

Mrs. Robins: Grazie, arrivederci.
Thank you, goodbye.

---

17. A LITTLE PRACTICE

a. Say you would like to change £350 and a Eurocheque.
b. Ask what the exchange rate is for sterling.

 STAMPS AND POSTCARDS

Andrew goes to a tobacconist (**il tabaccaio**) where he choses some postcards and asks for stamps and a phonecard.

Andrew: Queste tre cartoline e cinque francobolli per l'Inghilterra.
These three postcards and five stamps for England.

Tobacconist: I francobolli tutti per cartolina?
All the stamps for postcards?

Andrew: No, tre per cartolina e due per lettera.
No, three for postcards and two for letters.

Tobacconist: Le serve altro?
Anything else?

Andrew: Ah sì, una carta telefonica.
Oh yes, a telephone card.

Tobacconist: Da cinque o diecimila lire?
A five or ten thousand one?

Andrew: Da diecimila, grazie.
A ten thousand one, thanks.

HOW TO ... ask for 2 stamps for postcards/letters to Great Britain
due francobolli per cartolina/lettera per la Gran Bretagna

---

18. A LITTLE PRACTICE

a. Ask for four letter stamps for Great Britain.

b. Ask how much the postcards are.

CALLING HOME

Mrs. Robins wants to call home. She goes to a phone centre and asks for information about numbers and charges.

Mrs. Robins: Scusi, per telefonare in Gran Bretagna che prefisso devo fare?
Excuse me, what is the code for Great Britain?

Clerk: Zero-zero-quattro-quattro è il prefisso internazionale, poi deve fare il prefisso della città senza lo zero.
0044 is the international code, then you dial the area code without the zero.

Mrs. Robins: Quando comincia la tariffa ridotta?
When does the cheap rate start?

Clerk: Dalle ventidue alle otto nei giorni feriali e tutto il giorno la domenica.
From 10 p.m. to 8 a.m. on week days, all day long on Sundays.

Mrs. Robins: Se telefono da qui come devo pagare?
How can I pay if I call from here?

Clerk: Il telefono è a scatti; pagherà qui alla cassa, in contanti o con una carta di credito, dopo la telefonata.
The phone call is charged by units; you will pay here at the cashpoint, in cash or by credit card, once you have made your call.

Mrs. Robins: Grazie. Posso telefonare?
Thank you. Can I make a call?

Clerk: Si accomodi nella cabina numero sette.
From box number seven.

HOW TO... ask the international code for England
qual è il prefisso per l'Inghilterra?

ask to see London's telephone directory
potrei vedere l'elenco telefonico di Londra?

9. A LITTLE PRACTICE

a. You need to call home from Italy. Say the number, adding the international code – in Italian!

MONEY

Italian currency is the **lira**, abbreviated as **L.** or **Lit.** and divided into 1,000, 2,000, 5,000, 10,000, 50,000 and 100,000 lire notes and 50, 100, 200 and 500 lire coins. The telephone token, "**il gettone**", is worth 200 lire. Remember that in the Italian numeric system the comma becomes a dot: so "L100.000" is one hundred thousand lire!

To change money, Eurocheques or traveller's cheques, banks offer the best rates, but you can find exchange facilities, "**ufficio cambi**", elsewhere. At airports and in main town centres there are also 24-hour automatic change machines.

Banks are usually open Monday to Friday from 8.15 till 13.15 and in the early afternoon from 14.45 to 15.45. Some do a 9 to 5 day. They are all closed on Saturdays.

You can buy stamps at the tobacconist's, "**il tabaccaio**", which is easily recognizable by a big white T on a black background. If a bar bears the T sign it means that the shop sells cigarettes and stamps too. Of course you can find stamps at the post office, "**l'ufficio postale**", marked by a yellow sign with PT on it. Like many other public offices, post offices are generally open to the public from 8.30 till 13.30, and close a little earlier on Saturdays.

There are different stamp rates for different countries and the price depends on whether you are sending letters or postcards. When you want to buy stamps, therefore, you must state if you need "**francobolli per cartolina**", stamps for postcards, or "**per lettera**", for letters, and the country you want to send to.

Mailboxes are big, red boxes with one or two openings. If there are two, one will be "**per la città**", for mail addressed within the town, the other "**per tutte le altre destinazioni**", for every other destination. Special delivery services are available: there is "**l'espresso**", express mail, "**la raccomandata**", which guarantees delivery, for which there's also the "**ricevuta di ritorno**", a confirmation of delivery.

TELEPHONES

To call from a telephone box or booth you need coins (100, 200 and 500 lire only), telephone tokens, "**i gettoni**", or a telephone card, "**la carta telefonica**". Some phones also take telephone credit cards.

Some public phones, especially in bars or tobacconists' displaying a telephone sign, charge by the unit. You ask the tobacconist or barman to connect you ("**Mi può dare la linea, per favore?**") and after the call you ask how much it is – the tobacconist or barman reads the meter and you pay.

There are also some telephone centres, owned by SIP, the equivalent of BT, or other organizations, where you can find national and international telephone directories and coin or unit phones.

If you want to look up a number ask for "**l'elenco telefonico**", the telephone directory, or "**le pagine gialle**", the yellow pages. Otherwise, dial 12 for Directory Enquiries.

LANGUAGE NOTES

QUESTIONS

There are basically two main types of question-sentence in Italian. One type is rendered only by the rising intonation of the voice or, in written language, by the question mark; there's no change in word-order:

Sei inglese? (Are you English?)

A second type of question-sentence is that introduced by a "question-word", such as **Come?** (How, What), **Perché?** (Why), **Dove?** (Where), **Che cosa?** (What), etc:
Come ti chiami? (What's your name?)
Di dove sei? (Where are you from?)
Che cosa fai? (What do you do?)
Perché sei in Italia? (Why are you in Italy?)

7.1
Substitute the words in brackets in the following telephone conversation:

– **Pronto***?
– **Buongiorno**, (I'd like) **parlare** (with) **Marco**.
– **Chi parla?**
– **Sono Phil, un amico** (English).
– **Marco** (is) **fuori, tornerà verso le sette.**
– **Allora richiamerò** (later). **Arrivederci.**
– (Bye).

* When answering the phone **pronto** means "hello"; otherwise it means "ready".

7.2
Look at the postcard below.
a) Where is the sender writing from?
b) Is he alone?
c) What's the weather like?

VOCABULARY

la lira	the lira
la sterlina	the pound
Vorrei cambiare . . .	I'd like to change . . .
. . . in lire	. . . into liras
il cambio	the change rate
il tabaccaio	the tobacconist
una cartolina	a postcard
i francobolli	the stamps
la lettera	the letter
una carta telefonica	a telephone card
telefonare	to phone
il prefisso	the area code
la tariffa ridotta	cheap rate
il telefono a scatti	meter phone
in contanti	in cash
con carta di credito	by credit card
l'elenco telefonico	the telephone directory

8 Out for a Meal

When in Italy you will certainly have many opportunities to go out for a meal. This chapter will come in useful if you want to book a table in a restaurant, order a meal from the menu and ask for the bill!

ASKING FOR A TABLE

Sig. Lippi: Buonasera, ha un tavolo per tre?
Good evening, have you got a table for three?

Waitress: Questo tavolo in angolo va bene?
Is this table in the corner all right?

Sig. Lippi: Sì, grazie.
Yes, thank you.

Waitress: Accomodatevi. Vi porto subito il menu.
Take a seat. I will bring you the menu straightaway.

TRATTORIA DA MARCELLO

M E N U

Antipasti (*starters*)
crostini (*canapés*)
antipasto misto (*mixed starter*)

Primi piatti (*first courses*)
zuppa (*thick soup*)
spaghetti all'amatriciana (*spaghetti with tomato, onions, bacon*)
gnocchi al gorgonzola (*potato dumplings with blue cheese*)
tortellini in brodo (*tortellini in broth*)
piatto del giorno (*dish of the day*)

Secondi piatti
bistecca alla fiorentina (*grilled steak*)
abbacchio alla romana (*roast lamb*)
pollo alla cacciatora (*chicken casserole*)
vitella alla pizzaiola (*beef with tomato and mozzarella cheese*)

Contorni (*side dishes*)
patate arrosto (*roast potatoes*)
piselli (*peas*)
insalata mista (*mixed salad*)

Dessert
macedonia (*fruit salad*)
torta di mele (*apple pie*)
gelato (*ice cream*)

PLACING YOUR ORDER

Luke has just finished reading the trattoria menu. Let's see what he has ordered.

Waitress: Buongiorno, cosa le porto?
Good afternoon, what shall I bring you?

Luke: Dei crostini e, come primo, della zuppa.
"Crostini" and "zuppa" as first course.

Waitress: Come secondo?
As main course?

Luke: Cos'è l'abbacchio alla romana?
What is "abbacchio alla romana"?

Waitress: Agnello arrosto.
Roast lamb.

Luke: Allora abbacchio e, come contorno, insalata mista.
Then roast lamb and some mixed salad as a side dish.

Waitress: Da bere le consiglio il vino rosso della casa.
To drink I recommend the house red (wine).

Luke: Va bene, mezzo litro.
OK, half a litre.

OW TO . . .   ask if there is a free table for one/two/three . . .
Ha un tavolo per uno/due/tre . . . ?

order a dish for yourself
per me crostini

for someone else
per il signore . . .
per la signora . . .
per la signorina . . .
per i bambini . . . (the children)

ask what a particular dish is
cos'è l'abbacchio?

20. A LITTLE PRACTICE

a. You have spotted a nice place to eat. How would you ask if there is a table for three?

b. Now imagine you are at the "Trattoria da Marcello" with a friend. Read through the menu and order for both of you.

ASKING FOR THE BILL

Sig.ra Lippi: Mi può portare il conto per favore?
Can I have the bill, please?

Waiter: Sì, subito, signora.
Straightaway, madam.

Sig.ra Lippi: Posso pagare con una carta di credito?
Can I pay by credit card?

Waiter: Certamente.
Certainly.

Sig.ra Lippi: Può farmi una ricevuta?
Could you give me a receipt?

Waiter: Sì, eccola.
Here you are.

HOW TO... ask for the bill
Mi può portare il conto per favore?

---

21. A LITTLE PRACTICE

a. You have just enjoyed a lovely meal in a restaurant. Ask for the bill, and then ask the waiter if you can pay by credit card.

STREETWISE

A nice and inexpensive way of eating out is to go for a **pizza** in a **pizzeria**.

The variety of **pizza** is vast, as the original basic cheese and tomato topping now has many delicious variations.

Another typically Italian place to eat out is the **trattoria**. The **trattoria** specializes in **cucina casalinga** – rustic, often region dishes. Sometimes there isn't a written menu, the waiter will tell you what has been prepared for the day. The choice of dishes, even if it is not huge, will almost certainly include some **specialità della casa** (house specialities), which are worth trying. Avoid the **menu turistico**, a fixed menu which can be overpriced and far from adventurous. The wine is usually served **sfuso** ("loose"), in half litre (**mezzo litro**), three quarters (**tre quarti**) or one litre (**un litro**) jugs.

CEDENTE O PRESTATORE, DOMICILIO O RESIDENZA, CODICE FISCALE, PARTITA IVA

PIZZERIA MARTINO
di Lorenzetti Chiara & C. sas
Piazzetta de' Crocifisso n. 4
56125 PISA - Tel. 500016
C. F. e P. IVA 0103163 050 0

DATI IDENTIFICATIVI DEL CLIENTE

RICEVUTA FISCALE - FATTURA (RICEVUTA FISCALE) LEGGE 30.12.91 N. 413

QUANTITA	DESCRIZIONE	IMPORTO
5	COPERTI	12.500
3	VINO - BIRRA	11.000
1	ACQUA MINERALE	1.500
5	PIZZA	40.000
	ANTIPASTI	
	PRIMI PIATTI	
	SECONDI PIATTI	
	CONTORNI	
	FORMAGGI	
	FRUTTA	
	DOLCI - DESSERT	
	CAFFÈ - LIQUORI	
	PASTI A PREZZO FISSO	

CONTEGGIO IVA	Corrispettivo pagato	65.000
..........................%	Corrispettivo non pagato	
	TOTALE DOCUMENTO	65.000

DATE 1.9.93   NUMERO PROGRESSIVO 2607

ABR 109349/93

A TYPICAL MEAL

A typical meal at a restaurant or **trattoria** is usually composed of **antipasto** (starter), **primo piatto** (first course), **secondo piatto** (main course) and **contorno** (side dish), sometimes **formaggio** (cheese) and **frutta** (fruit), and finally **dolce** (dessert). Of course you do not have to order every single **portata** (course); it is quite common to skip the main course and go from the first one to the **dolce** or to have only a main course and side dish and maybe a dessert.

Service charge is nearly always included. You are therefore not expected to leave a tip.

LANGUAGE NOTES

AVERE (TO HAVE)

io ho	I have
tu hai	you have (informal)
lui ha	he has
lei ha	she has
lei ha	you have (formal)
noi abbiamo	we have
voi avete	you have (plural)
loro hanno	they have

ho un cane = I have a dog
ho due fratelli = I have two brothers

Please note:
ho fame = I am hungry
ho trent'anni = I am thirty years old

8.1

You are in the "Pizzeria Pulcinella". Read through the pizza menu below and place your own order.

PIZZA:

MARGHERITA (mozzarella cheese and tomato)
AI FUNGHI (mushrooms)
CAPRICCIOSA (mozzarella, tomato, ham and olives)
QUATTRO STAGIONI (mozzarella, tomato, artichokes, anchovies and olives)
AI QUATTRO FORMAGGI (four different cheeses)
CALZONE (a type of stuffed pancake)

8.2

You normally don't eat meat, so what can you order?

1. come primo   a) zuppa
   (as a first course) b) spaghetti all'amatriciana
                        c) tortellini in brodo

2. come secondo   a) abbacchio alla romana
   (as a main course)   b) vitella alla pizzaiola
                        c) pesce al forno

3. come contorno   a) patate arrosto
   (as a side dish)   b) piselli
                        c) insalata mista

VOCABULARY

il ristorante	the restaurant
il cameriere	the waiter
la cameriera	the waitress
il menu	the menu
l'antipasto	the starter
il primo	the first course
il secondo	the main course
il dolce	the dessert
il vino bianco/rosso	white/red wine
il sale	the salt
il pepe	the pepper
per me	for me
Cos'è . . . ?	What is . . . ?
Cosa c'è nel . . . ?	What's in the . . . ?
il conto	the bill
il coperto	cover charge
il servizio	service charge
la mancia	the tip

9 Shopping

Andrew wants to buy something nice for his mother. He enters a gift-shop, invitingly called "**La scatola magica**" (the magic box).

BUYING A PRESENT

Shop assistant: Buonasera.
Good evening.

Andrew: Devo fare un regalo e . . .
I want to buy a present and . . .

Shop assistant: Quanto vuole spendere?
How much would you like to spend?

Andrew: Sulle quarantamila lire.
Around forty thousand lire.

Shop assistant: È per una signora?
Is it for a woman?

Andrew: Sì, per mia madre.
Yes, for my mother.

Shop assistant: Abbiamo questi bei fermalibri . . .
We have these beautiful book-ends . . .

Andrew: Mmm. Ne ha già uno simile. Vorrei qualcosa di particolare.
Mmm. She's got something similar. I'd like something special.

Shop assistant: Allora forse questo cupido in terracotta?
Then perhaps this terracotta Cupid?

Andrew: Ah sì, questo le piacerebbe molto. Quanto costa?
Oh yes, she'd love that. How much is it?

Shop assistant: È un pochino più caro. Viene cinquantacinquemila lire.
It's slightly more expensive. It's 55,000 lire.

89

Andrew: Va bene. Mi può fare una confezione regalo, p[
favore?
That's OK. Can you wrap it for me, please?

HOW TO... say you want to buy a present for . . .
Devo fare un regalo a . . .

say that you don't want to spend more than . . .
Non voglio spendere più di . . .

you want to spend about twenty thousand lire
Vorrei spendere sulle ventimila lire

ask to have your purchase nicely wrapped
Mi può fare una confezione regalo, per favore?

---

22. A LITTLE PRACTICE

a. You want to buy a present for your wife/husband/friend.
What would you say to the shop assistant?

b. Say you want to spend around fifty thousand lire.

LOOKING FOR SHOES

Mrs. Robins would like to buy a pair of Italian shoes. It's **sal(**
(sale) time and something has caught her eye in a shop
window . . .

Mrs. Robins: Vorrei vedere i mocassini marroni che sono in
vetrina.
I'd like to see the brown loafers in the window.

Shop assistant: Quelli in camoscio con la fibbia?
The suede ones with the buckle?

Mrs. Robins: Sì.
Yes.

Shop assistant: Che numero?
Which size?

Mrs. Robins: Credo trentasette.
37 I think.

[*She tries them on*]

Mrs. Robins:	No, queste sono piccole.	
	No, these are too small.	
Shop assistant:	Provi il trentotto.	
	Try size 38.	
Mrs. Robins:	Ah sì, queste vanno meglio. Sono scontate?	
	Oh yes, these fit better. Are they in the sale?	
Shop assistant:	Sì, c'è il trenta per cento di sconto, vengono sessantanovemila lire.	
	Yes, there is 30% discount, they are 69,000 lire.	
Mrs. Robins:	Le prendo.	
	I'll take them.	

HOW TO…   say you want to see some black/low-heeled/high-heeled shoes
Vorrei vedere delle scarpe nere/senza tacco/con il tacco

say you are size 37/43
Ho il 37/43

say the shoes are fine
Vanno bene
say they are small/big/tight
Sono piccole/grandi/strette

The following conversion table for shoe sizes may be useful:

UK		Italy
4½–5	=	38
5½–6	=	39
6½	=	40
7	=	41
7½	=	42
8½	=	43
9½	=	44
10½	=	45
11	=	46

SHOPPING FOR FRUIT AND VEGETABLES
Andrew is passing by a busy and colourful fruit and veg
market. He decides to buy something from the **frutta e
verdura** (fruit and vegetables) stalls.

 Greengrocer: Guardate che pesche! Due e quattro al chilo!
     *Look, what nice peaches! Two (thousand) and four
     (lire) a kilo!*

 Andrew: Scusi, quanto vengono le pesche?
     Excuse me, how much are the peaches?

 Greengrocer: Duemilaquattrocento lire al chilo.
     Two thousand and four hundred lire a kilo.

 Andrew: Me ne dia mezzo chilo.
     Give me half a kilo, please.

 Greengrocer: Altro?
     Anything else?

 Andrew: No, basta così.
     No, that's all.

 Andrew: Quanto costano i carciofi?
     How much are the artichokes?

 Greengrocer: Mille lire l'uno.
     One thousand lire each.

 Andrew: Me ne dia una decina.
     Give me ten (of them), please.

 Greengrocer: Questi sono buoni da mangiare in pinzimonio
     Ecco a lei. Le serve altro?
     *These are delicious to eat with an oil, salt and pepp
     dip. Here you are. Anything else?*

Andrew: Vorrei dei pomodori.	**FRUTTA**
I'd like some tomatoes.	**VERDURA**
Greengrocer: Di questi qui vanno bene?	**SPERANZA M.**

Andrew: Vorrei dei pomodori.
I'd like some tomatoes.
Greengrocer: Di questi qui vanno bene?
Are these OK?
Andrew: Sì, un chilo, per favore.
Yes, one kilo, please.

```
FRUTTA
VERDURA
SPERANZA M.
REC N.2962-A
CCIAA LIVORNO
P.I.00773290499


REP-04
        +      2.500

N.ARTIC.   0001

TOTALE   2.500


CONT.TE  2.500
RESTO        0
#0039
03/09/93 10-26
MF AW 85001348
```

HOW TO ... say you would like a kilo of apples/
potatoes . . .
(Vorrei) un chilo di mele/patate . . .

ask how much are they per kilo
Quanto costano al chilo?

say that's all you want
Basta così, grazie

3. A LITTLE PRACTICE
a. You want to buy half a kilo of tomatoes.
What would you say?
b. Ask if they have any eggs.

STREETWISE

SHOPS

Shops usually open from 9 till 12.30 and again from 15.30 to
19.30, and slightly later in the summer. They are closed on
Monday mornings, except for food shops, which usually close
on Wednesday afternoons. Some shops and supermarkets are
open all day.

In mid-August many shops and bars are closed, giving a
deserted atmosphere to most towns, except the tourist resorts.
Those shops and bars which close during the holiday period
usually have a sign on the door stating "**chiuso per ferie**".

LANGUAGE NOTES

QUANTO COSTA/COSTANO?

Quanto costa? means "How much is it?"
Quanto costano? means "How much are they?"

So, if you want to ask "How much is the room?", you will say "**Quanto costa la camera?**", and if you want to say "How much are the rooms?", you will say "**Quanto costano le camere?**".

Note that **quanto** remains the same in both cases, because in both cases it translates "how much".

QUANTO/QUANTA/QUANTI/QUANTE

Sometimes, however, you will have to use different forms, according to the gender and number. If you want to say "how many", you will have to use **quanti** or **quante** as in the example below:

quanti siete?   (how many are you?)
per quante notti?   (for how many nights)

YOUR TURN

9.1
Where would you buy the following items?

francobolli	edicola
gelato	bar
scarpe	farmacia
aspirina	tabaccaio
giornale	fioraio
cartoline	macelleria

There is one item you won't be able to find in any of the above shops.

9.2
You would like to buy a leather bag. What would you ask the shop assistant?

VOCABULARY

la commessa	the shop assistant (f.)
il commesso	the shop assistant (m.)
Posso dare un'occhiata?	Can I have a browse?
un regalo	a present
spendere	to spend
(più) caro	(more) expensive
in vetrina	in the window
Che numero?	Which size?
i saldi	the sales
1 chilo	1 kilo
mezzo chilo	half a kilo
l'uno	each
Altro?	Anything else?
le uova	eggs

10 Emergency!

In this last chapter you will find some information and hints that will come in useful in an emergency situation.

Mrs. Robins has just had her bag stolen. She is now **in questura** (at the police headquarters), talking to a policeman.

AL LADRO!
Stop thief!

> *Policeman:* Come è successo?
> *What happened?*
>
> *Mrs. Robins:* Stavo camminando in via Roma, guardando le vetrine, quando mi sono sentita tirare la borsa. Non ce l'ho fatta a trattenerla e me l'hanno portata via. Erano due ragazzi in vespa.
> *I was walking down via Roma, doing a bit of window shopping, when I felt someone pulling at my bag. I wasn't able to keep hold of it and they pulled it off. They were two young men on a scooter.*

Policeman: I soliti scippatori! È fortunata che non l'hanno spinta a terra o malmenata.
Scooter-riding purse-snatchers! You are lucky they didn't push you to the ground or beat you up.

Mrs. Robins: Sì, proprio fortunata.
Yes, really lucky.

Policeman: Cosa aveva nella borsa?
What did you have in your bag?

Mrs. Robins: Tutto: portafoglio, carte di credito, passaporto. E le chiavi della mia casa in Gran Bretagna.
Everything: my purse, credit cards, passport. And the keys to my house in Britain.

Policeman: Ha telefonato alla sua banca per le carte di credito?
Have you called your bank to cancel the credit cards?

Mrs. Robins: Sì, sì, è la prima cosa che ho fatto.
Oh yes, that's the first thing I did.

Policeman: Non le resta che firmare la denuncia e sperare che si ritrovi qualcosa. Ma ne dubito.
Now you must sign your statement and hope that something will be found. Although I doubt it.

HOW TO...   say your bag has been stolen
mi hanno rubato la borsa

say your purse/wallet has been stolen
mi hanno rubato il portafoglio

---

24. A LITTLE PRACTICE

a. How would you say your car has been stolen?

SOMEONE NEEDS A DOCTOR

It's late at night. Andrew is in his hotel room with a friend who is not feeling very well. Actually he's feeling rather sick. Andrew goes to the reception and asks to see a doctor.

Andrew: Il mio amico nella camera dodici si sente male. Dove posso trovare un medico?
My friend in room 12 is sick. Where can I find a doctor?

Porter: Chiamo la guardia medica.
I can phone the doctor on night duty.

[The porter talks to the doctor.]

Porter: Che sintomi ha il suo amico?
What are the symptoms?

Andrew: Ha vomitato più volte, ha diarrea ed è quasi svenuto.
He's been sick several times, he's got diarrhoea and he nearly fainted.

Porter: Il medico dice che sarà qui al più presto. Potrebbe trattarsi di intossicazione alimentare. Torni dal suo amico e stia con lui finché il medico di guardia non arriva.
The doctor says that he'll be here as soon as possible. It could be food poisoning. Go back to your friend and stay with him until the doctor arrives.

Andrew: La ringrazio infinitamente.
Thank you ever so much.

Porter: Verrò su tra poco a vedere se ha bisogno di qualcosa.
I'll be upstairs in a minute to see if you need anything.

Andrew: Va bene, grazie ancora per il suo aiuto.
OK, thank you very much for your help.

say you need a doctor
Ho bisogno di un medico/dottore

say you are on antibiotics
Sto prendendo degli antibiotici

ask for an ambulance
C'è bisogno di un'ambulanza

25. A LITTLE PRACTICE

a. You witnessed an accident and you call the emergency service. How would you say you need an ambulance?

BREAKDOWN

Mrs. Robins has had a breakdown on the motorway. She dials 116 for the **Soccorso ACI** (AA/RAC) from one of the emergency telephones.

Mrs. Robins: Ho un guasto alla macchina. Potete aiutarmi?
My car has broken down. Can you help me?

Operatore: Dove si trova?
Where are you?

Mrs. Robins: Sono sulla Firenze Mare, al km. centotrentotto.
I am on the motorway "Firenze Mare", km. 138.

Operatore: Che tipo di vettura ha?
What make is your car?

Mrs. Robins: Un'Opel Corsa presa a noleggio.
It's a hired Opel Corsa.

Operatore: Il numero di targa?
Registration number?

Mrs. Robins: FIM39851.

Operatore: Mandiamo subito qualcuno. Resti vicino all'auto.
We'll send someone straightaway. Stay by the car.

Mrs. Robins: Grazie.
Thank you.

STREETWISE

POLICE

If you need the police in an emergency, dial **113**. Otherwise go to **la questura** (police headquarters).

DOCTOR AND CHEMIST'S

If you need a doctor or dentist you can go to the local health unit **USL** (**Unità Sanitaria Locale**). In case of an emergency go to the **Pronto Soccorso** (Casualty) of the nearest **ospedale** (hospital). If you need an **ambulance**, dial the emergency services number **113**. In many resorts there is **Guardia medica**, where a doctor is always on call. For minor matters you can go to a chemist's, marked with a red or green cross. They keep usual shop hours, and all of them display a list of chemists on night and holiday duty (**Farmacie di turno**) outside.

BREAKDOWNS

If you break down call **ACI** (**Automobil Club d'Italia**), the equivalent of AA and RAC, on **116**. You will be asked where you are, what make your car is and the registration number (**numero di targa**). On the motorway there are orange emergency telephones marked **SOS**. If you have an accident, call the police.

LANGUAGE NOTES

NEGATIVES

For once, it couldn't be easier. To make a negative sentence, just put **non** (not) in front of the verb:

fumo (I smoke)
non fumo (I don't smoke)
ho chiamato Marco (I called Marco)
non ho chiamato Marco (I didn't call Marco)

YOUR TURN

10.1

a) You are in "Piazza Roma". There's been an accident and someone needs an ambulance. What number would you dial? What would you say?
b) How would you say your bag has been stolen?
c) How would you say that your car doesn't start?

VOCABULARY

aiuto!	help!
il dottore/medico	the doctor
il dentista	the dentist
la farmacia	the chemist's
l'ambulanza	the ambulance
l'ospedale	the hospital
mi sento male	I am sick/ill
un guasto	breakdown
un guasto al motore	engine failure
l'autorimessa	the garage
l'incidente	the accident
il soccorso stradale	(road) breakdown assistance
la polizia	the police
perdere	to loose
rubare	to steal

Key to Exercises

In this Key there will be times when we've given just one of
several possible answers – as for example in chapter 2, practice
1, question a).

CHAPTER 2

1. A LITTLE PRACTICE
a. Un tè al latte e un cappuccino, per favore.
b. Quant'è?

2. A LITTLE PRACTICE
a. Un caffè e un tramezzino, per favore.
b. Un tè al limone e una pizzetta, per favore. Ecco lo scontrino.

3. A LITTLE PRACTICE
a. Un'aranciata e una birra, per favore.
b. Cosa prendi? Un bicchiere di vino bianco e un martini, per favore.

YOUR TURN
2.1
a. (ii) Un'aranciata.
b. (i) Un panino.
c. (ii) Una cioccolata calda.
2.2
– Un bicchiere d'acqua, per favore.
– Gassata.

CHAPTER 3

4. A LITTLE PRACTICE
a. Avete una camera singola con bagno?
b. Quanto costa?
c. È possibile vedere la camera?

5. A LITTLE PRACTICE
a. Siamo in tre, due ragazze e un ragazzo, avete posto per stanotte?
b. A che ora chiudete la sera?

6. A LITTLE PRACTICE
a. Siamo in tre, con una macchina e una tenda. Avete posto?
b. Quant'è al giorno?

3.1

a/3; b/2; c/1.

3.2 (ON TAPE)

a) true

b) true

c) false

d) false

3.3

– Avete posto?

– Per tre.

– Due.

3.4

a) There isn't any hot water.

b) Here is the key, room 18.

c) A place in the shade.

d) Can you prepare my bill, please?

e) Breakfast is included.

f) How much is it for a week?

g) I'll be leaving tomorrow.

CHAPTER 4

7. A LITTLE PRACTICE

a. Mi chiamo . . .

b. Come si chiama? (formal)

Come ti chiami? (informal)

8. A LITTLE PRACTICE

a. Sono . . .

9. A LITTLE PRACTICE

a. Giorgio, questo è Paul. Paul, ti presento Giorgio.

b. Signor Bandini le presento il Signor Jones. Signor Jones le presento il Signor Bandini.

10. A LITTLE PRACTICE

a. Sono di . . .

b. Di dov'è? (formal)

Di dove sei? (informal)

YOUR TURN

4.1

– Come ti chiami?

– Sei inglese?

– Sono italiana.

– Di dove?

4.2
a) Lei è scozzese?
b) (Io) Abito a Edimburgo.
c) Lei è inglese, e simpatica.
d) Tu sei di Londra.
e) Questo è mio fratello Andrew.

CHAPTER 5

11. A LITTLE PRACTICE
a. Scusi, dov'è l'Ente del Turismo?
   Scusi, dov'è la stazione?
   Scusi, dov'è il duomo?
12. A LITTLE PRACTICE
a. Scusi, per andare al Consolato Britannico?

YOUR TURN
5.1
You are going to the station, **alla stazione**.

5.2
– Scusi, per andare al Palazzo dei Congressi?
– È lontano?
– Grazie.

CHAPTER 6

13. A LITTLE PRACTICE
a. Scusi, qual è l'autobus per la stazione?
b. Dove devo scendere per la stazione?
14. A LITTLE PRACTICE
a. Alla stazione, per favore.
b. Quant'è per andare alla stazione?
c. Mi può fare una ricevuta?
15. A LITTLE PRACTICE
a. Due biglietti di sola andata per Roma.
b. Scusi, a che ora parte il treno per Roma?
c. Scusi, da che binario parte il treno per Roma?
16. A LITTLE PRACTICE
a. Quanto costa noleggiare un'auto per una settimana?
b. L'assicurazione è compresa nel prezzo?

6.1
a) qual è
numero
b) la fermata
fronte
c) la linea
la
d) per

6.2
Quattro biglietti per la Stazione Centrale, per favore.

CHAPTER 7

17. A LITTLE PRACTICE
a. Vorrei cambiare trecentocinquanta sterline e un eurocheque.
b. Quant'è il cambio per la sterlina?
18. A LITTLE PRACTICE
a. Quattro francobolli per lettera per la Gran Bretagna.
b. Quanto costano le cartoline?
19. A LITTLE PRACTICE
a. zero zero quattro quattro . . .

YOUR TURN
7.1
vorrei
con
inglese
è
più tardi
Arrivederci
7.2
a) Florence
b) He's with some friends
c) Wonderful

CHAPTER 8

20. A LITTLE PRACTICE
a. Ha un tavolo per tre?
b. Per la signora/il signore gnocchi al gorgonzola e bistecca alla fiorentina. Per me spaghetti all'amatriciana e pollo alla cacciatora con contorno di piselli.
21. A LITTLE PRACTICE
a. Mi porta il conto, per favore.
Posso pagare con una carta di credito?

8.1
Una pizza ai quattro formaggi, per favore.
8.2
1. zuppa
2. pesce al forno
3. tutti e tre (all three are possible)

CHAPTER 9

22. A LITTLE PRACTICE
a. Vorrei fare un regalo a mia moglie/a mio marito/a un amico.
b. Vorrei spendere sulle cinquantamila lire.
23. A LITTLE PRACTICE
a. Mezzochilo di pomodori, per favore.
b. Ha delle uova?

YOUR TURN
9.1

francobolli	tabaccaio
gelato	bar
aspirina	farmacia
giornale	edicola
cartoline	tabaccaio or bar

You need to go to a "negozio di calzature" to find "le scarpe".

YOUR TURN
9.2
Vorrei vedere una borsa di pelle, per favore.

CHAPTER 10

24. A LITTLE PRACTICE
a. Mi hanno rubato l'auto.
25. A LITTLE PRACTICE
a. C'è bisogno di un'ambulanza.

YOUR TURN
10.1
a) 113.
C'è stato un incidente, mandate subito un'ambulanza in Piazza Roma.
b) Mi hanno rubato la borsa.
c) La mia auto non parte.

Mini-Dictionary

A

a at, to
abbigliamento clothes
accanto a next to
l'aceto vinegar
l'acqua water
    a. potabile drinking water
    a. gassata fizzy mineral water
    a. naturale still mineral water
    un'acqua tonica a tonic water
l'aereo plane
l'aeroporto airport
un adulto an adult
l'agenzia di viaggi travel agency
l'aglio garlic
l'agnello lamb
aiuto! help!
l'albergo hotel
l'albicocca apricot
l'alimentari grocer's
l'altro, a the other (one)
allora then
l'ambasciata embassy
l'ambulanza ambulance
americano, a American
anche also, too
andare to go
andata e ritorno return
l'angolo corner
l'anno year

l'antipasto starter
l'aperitivo aperitif
l'appuntamento appointment; date
l'arancia orange
l'aranciata orangeade
l'aria condizionata air-conditioning
arrivederci goodbye
assente absent
l'assicurazione insurance
attenzione caution; attention
australiano, a Australian
l'autista driver
l'autobus bus
l'autonoleggio car hire
l'autostrada motorway
l'autorimessa garage
avanti go

B

il bagaglio luggage
il bagno bathroom
il bambino/la bambina child
la banca bank
il banco counter
il bar bar
il barbiere barber
il/la barista barman/barmaid
basta that's enough, that's all
bello, a beautiful

bene well
   va bene that's OK
   benissimo very well
la benzina petrol
il benzinaio petrol station
bere to drink
le bevande drinks
bianco white
il bicchiere glass
la biglietteria ticket office
il biglietto ticket
il binario platform
la birra beer
la bistecca steak
la borsa bag
la bottiglia bottle
una brioche croissant, bun
britannico, a British
la buca delle lettere letter-box
buonanotte good night
buonasera good evening
buongiorno good morning
buono, a good
   buonissimo very good
il burro butter

C

la cabina telefonica phone box
il caffè coffee
   caffè macchiato white coffee
la caldaia boiler
caldo hot, warm
cambiare to change
il cambio exchange rate
la camera bedroom
   c. singola/doppia single/double
     room
   c. matrimoniale room with
     double bed
il cameriere waiter
la cameriera waitress
il campeggio/camping camp site
il cappuccino cappuccino
il carciofo artichoke
la carne meat
caro, a expensive; dear

la carta di credito credit card
la carta d'identità identity card
la carta telefonica telephone card
la cartolina postcard
la casa home, house
la cassa checkout; cash desk
c'è there is, is there
cento one hundred
il centro centre
certo, certamente certainly
che that; which, what
chiamarsi to be called
   mi chiamo my name is
la chiave key
la chiesa church
un chilo a kilo
chilometraggio mileage
chiuso, a closed
ciao hi, hello; bye
cinquanta fifty
cinque five
la cioccolata chocolate
la città town, city
la coca-cola coke
il cognome surname
la coincidenza connection
la colazione breakfast
come how; as
il commesso/la commessa shop
   assistant
completo full
   al completo fully booked
compreso, a included
con with
conoscere to know; to meet
contanti cash
   in contanti in cash
il conto bill
il coperto cover charge
cosa what; **la cosa** thing

D

da from
una decina ten
il dentista dentist
desidera? Can I help you?